I0415568

• • • •

Text Copyright © 2013 by Stephen Paul West

Cover Design Copyright © 2013 by Stephen Paul West

Purchase copies on the Web. www.amazon.com

Visit the Author at: www.StephenPaulWest.com

LIBRARY OF CONGRESS CATALOGING-IN-PUBLICATION DATA

West, Stephen Paul
Extortion Politics and the Federal Shutdown / Stephen Paul West
p. cm.

Summary: Political Satire about the crazy and abstract ideology that a handful of zealots embrace that forced the American Government to shut down. Strangely, the humor contains a deep analysis of who is the true puppeteer behind the crippling shutdown.

• • • •

Extortion Politics and the Federal Shutdown

Blackmail of Lady Liberty – A Political Satire

Stephen Paul West

The mighty United States of America brought to a halt by a zealous group with a narrow agenda of absolute control. Is this a plot for a new conspiracy movie? Is this the act of foreign terrorists?

No. Sigh… it is the act of Michele Bachmann and 49 others to extort the nation into obeying the edict of the Tea Party Caucus.

Good political satire is satisfying and exposing of naked truths. And, nothing is more naked than the 'truths' that Grover Norquist wants to teach the nation. He is simply using his favorite puppet – Michele Bachmann and the Tea Party as a smoke screen to punish us all.

If you want to know the REAL reason for the Federal shutdown, this books has the crop-circles of reality. The single little circle of vindictive control is in the shape of a lobbyist's head. Grover Norquist is that tiny crop-circle. No aliens, terrorists or conspiracy required to shut down the Federal Government. Just ego and dimwitted oppression.

Can't we all agree to just throw away this twisted, ugly, uptight little pirate called Norquist? Lady Liberty should never be blackmailed into a narrow, non-functional solution as dictated by a lobbyist.

Extortion Politics and the Federal Shutdown

Blackmail of Lady Liberty – A Political Satire

Chapters

Extortion Politics

CHAPTER 1

A HighJacked Nation

Normally, it wouldn't be possible to highjack an entire nation like Somali pirates grabbing a fishing boat. Countries are kind of big things. And, where do you throw the grabbling hooks?

Well, nation hijacking is solved by a little group of 49 legislators who take their orders from a single Lobbyist.

> **"Capt'n Lobbyist if ya please. Arrrr,
> Capt'n Lobbyist Grover Norquist."**

Strangely, Michele Bachman serves as first mate. She isn't exactly Smee smart, either. Heck, she isn't any kind of smart. But, this is just the kind of blank slate that pirate scum need.

No scruples and no brains desired.

And Cap'n Norquist got twice as much as he bargain for with Michele Bachman and the band of <u>Tea Party Caucus</u>*

*real name. Also, I love the caucus-ian part of that little group. Kind of Freudian of them. (sub-text Tea Party Caucasians. Cute.)

Michele Bachmann admits she 'doesn't understand it all' but it doesn't stop her from having an agenda bigger than it all.

I can't believe she actually likes this 'blank slate' photo, and uses it as an official image. This makes writing satire almost too easy. I should blush at not having to use any Photoshop to master her absolute gaze of ignorant unknowing. But, this is her. And she actually LIKES this picture.

Tea Party Caucus — well, it's a juvenile website with 4 pages of information. One of those pages is a link to the Constitution and Declaration of Independence, although these politicians demonstrate absolute ignorance of any of the text. They just hold the idea of those documents sacred; not the messy application of freedom for everybody.

Anyway, I know some 8 year-olds with more advanced WordPress blogs on Lego construction then the Tea Party Caucus website has for national governance. Go ahead and look, maybe they will improve the website after my little book. God knows they have the money for it:

http://teapartycaucus-bachmann.house.gov/

Yet, these simpletons – lead by Michele Bachmann?!? – are gonna dang straight teach the nation sumthin'.

Really, how in the green earth, does Michele Bachmann get to run anything. She is not bright enough to arrange a community garage sale (my apologies to community garage sales everywhere).

The answer is the simple-minded control of a simple-minded, but mean-spirited lobbyist — Mr. Grover Norquist.

Yes, a lobbyist is in charge of a nation. He is in-charge because he bought 49 ignorant Senators and Representatives breakfast. The breakfast part isn't satire, nor, an exaggeration.

This motley crew of Tea Party thugs sold out the nation because of breakfasting with Grover Norquist.

More on this later.

● ● ● ●

Quick!

How many Tea Party Caucus members does it take to screw in a lightbulb?

Trick question. You have to deregulate utilities companies first, and then let the market decide a new standard for electricity. Then the electricity has to be sold by brokers. Also, the mandate for fluorescent lights needs to be repealed. Then and only then, will a Tea Party Caucus member have the maid change the light-bulb.

Actually, I'll revisit the history of electricity because it carries some weight for the United States as the Federal Government dies a painful death at the hands of 49 people

Oh, by the way. Grover Norquist often boasted:

> **"I'm not in favor of abolishing the government. I just want to shrink it down to the size where we can drown it in the bathtub."**

It is strange to me that a handful of zealots <u>in the government</u> hate and scorn the government in which they work. This is a self-loathing denoting the minds of true psychopaths.

Anyway, remember when America didn't have electricity from coast to coast? Well, imagine if it didn't. That was the story only 90 years ago, and many political foes fought to leave the nation in darkness.

The entire 'rural electrification' discussion is germane because the issue of shutting down our modern government over a social benefit program is the same argument fought 90 years ago.

It was '*electricity benefits*' 90 years ago. Today it is '*health care benefits*'. The point of either battle was simply because some thugs hate ANY kind of social benefit at all. Electricity or Health. (Ms. Bachmann – germane does not mean German. It means relevant… er… useful.)

• • • •

However, rather than opposing rural electrification, the new battle ground is the 'Affordable Care Act'. Keep in mind it is already a law. It is also known as ACA, and alternately by Obamacare – although it was actually Mitt Romney who drafted the plan, but who's counting.

Wait! I'm a political humorist and I'm counting! It was Mitt Romney! But I digress.

ACA is already a law. That means, it is already a law.

The House and Senate ALREADY passed the bill. The President ALREADY signed it into law. And the Courts have ALREADY upheld the law.

The Republicans position is shutting down the government must be done to throw out this law. Well, no. That is blackmail.

I don't disagree that a balance budget is important. BUT THEY HAD YEARS TO WORK THAT OUT!!!

I understand the logistical application of the ACA law is a valid question. I personally think the lack of cost controls and regulations on hospitals present a huge potential for corruption. Until hospitals are forced to stop charging $3431 dollars for 3 hours in an emergency room because a little child has a 104 F fever after normal business hours. The hospital's total investment in health care was two chairs for the parents to sit in until the fever broke, and 5 Pediasure popsicles (all true).

This over-charging by the health care industry is a real problem. However, that is another problem separate from GIVING people access to health care in the first place.

What if the child actually had lethal meningitis and they did not take the child to the hospital. The child goes to school ill with flu-like symptoms. The next day 50 kids are on death's door.

Healthcare is in society's best interest because contagious diseases WANT humans to not get treatment. The Tea Party Caucus is actually on the side of parasites and virulent plagues. That should be a clue.

So, cost controls need to be discusses seriously. A balanced budget should be a serious discussion. In fact, both these issues needed to be resolved a long time ago. Taking the nation hostage, to deprive people of easy access to health care is stupid. But, that's the reason Ms. Bachmann is so aggressive about her position. Stupid is as stupid does.

● ● ● ●

I really want a balanced budget. I want responsible government.

However, I am not allowed to drive to Washington and take the Capital by force of blackmail.

I have to play by the rules.

Those rules are called LAW.

Affordable Care Act is already LAW.

Those 49 pirates of Norquist actually had a little experiment in hijacking political systems earlier. These thugs managed to steal the Republican Party about a year before the Federal shutdown.

Once that scurvy crew mastered kidnapping a political party, they had the brute experience on how to take the nation.

Therefore a faction of the GOP redefines Constitutional

methodology of bills becoming laws, by shutting down the government. Notice the GOP doesn't say the solution isn't raising the debt ceiling. Ultimately, that is the only solution, even if ACA never existed.

Instead of democracy, though, 49 legislators are trying to void a law by blackmail. The Tea Party Caucus seized the budget, whereby a bunch of pirates blackmailed the ENTIRE nation to force a death to a law they don't like. This behavior is certainly not democracy. This is tyranny.

It's just like dead-beat dads who put paying child-support on a condition that only they get. Like "she can't use child support to buy a new car." Well, the courts don't operate like that. Neither do households where child-support is necessary. It is simple. The courts order the guy to pay, without any conditions, such as visitation rights, spending, or other factors. Still, some idiots make-up a rule outside of the law; and try to skirt paying for their own kids. That logic isn't logic at all. It's just a power-grab, and should result in arrests and jail time.

This Tea Party Caucus is no different. They don't like a rule, so they make a condition that obstructs obeying the rule. The sad and tragic part is it only took 49 of these blackmailers to seize the Republican Party, and then to seize the USA. Naturally, if allowed to continue, they will harm the entire global economy with a crisis of epic proportions. Ah, they do love drama.

● ● ● ●

Hey! I have 490 feet of rope to hang these clowns.

If necessary, I am willing to weave the rope out of grass with my bare hands as I go east to Washington D.C. That's the kind *'no guv-mint'* pioneer justice these simpletons seek. I say let's give it to them.

Seriously, the solution is just 49 people, 10 feet of rope each. According to my math....wait.... I'm forgetting Grover Norquist.

Anyway, the solution to the problem is only 10 feet of rope, perhaps reused 50 times to save costs.

My proposition is a good deal. America gets these monkeys out of Liberty's purse, and we can all get back to making the nation function. Why isn't my idea of forced coercion as legitimate as the Tea Party Caucus extortion of legislated law?

● ● ● ●

I realize there are some who will say that 49 people are not the problem. Well, I agree. It is 49 <u>legislators</u>, and, one <u>lobbyist</u>.

However, if I'm generous with the numbers I agree there might be even 100 Tea Party Caucus legislators who are forcing a nation into shutdown and brinksmanship of default.

I am not just an author. I am also a voter. In fact, I am an independent voter. I have voted for Republicans… in the past. But, the serious lack of control in the Republican party is stomach churning. What a bunch of limp Boehners. And nothing is as useless as a limp Boehner. When a Boehner can't whip a party into shape, well it's time for the party to turn off the lights and just go home.

For some reason the Republican party just doesn't have the guts to stand up to these Tea Party Caucus cry-babies (my apology to Boehner who is the cry-baby champion of the world).

The fight isn't about principles.

The fight is about ideology.

The danger is that ideology can be a really, really, really, sinister thing. Ideology can embrace a cosmos of good things, while hiding the sole kernel of absolute evil. However, when the core is evil, than the entire system is evil — even good sounding stuff like 'family values'.

Witness.... oh... I don't know. How about the United States government being shut down by 49 legislators with delusions of grandiose ideology.

The Chair of the Tea Party Caucus, Ms. Michele Bachmann said it best:

> *"We're not the mouthpiece. We are not taking the Tea Party and controlling it from Washington, D.C. We are also not here to vouch for the Tea Party or to vouch for any Tea Party organizations*

> *or to vouch for any individual people or*
> *actions, or billboards or signs or*
> *anything of the Tea Party. We are the*
> *receptacle."*

Yep. Michele is not the mouthpiece. She is the receptacle. *snicker*

But, her mouthpiece is all up inside this here government shut down. And her receptacle is getting serviced by a lobbyist named Grover Norquist.

● ● ● ●

Some may point out the 'in-fighting' between Michele Bachmann, Ted Cruz and Grover Norquist, and other Tea Party bigots. They are certainly snarky with each other — but only when each one gets MORE national coverage than the next.

These are vindictive, tiny-minded, narcissists.

They will always behave like vindictive, tiny-minded, narcissists.

Like all diagnosed narcissist they rage at each other when one gets more attention. However, just like little drops of toxic mercury they will snap back together when good things push them around.

If they are not all on the same team, then why did Ted Cruz and Michele Bachmann BOTH sign the Norquist Pledge? If you are an enemy to somebody why sign your soul away to them? Well, the enemy of my enemy is my friend.

Grover Norquist hold the lead-rope on Cruz and Bachmann even if those two are not smart enough to understand that fact.

● ● ● ●

Let me show a chart of ideology. The red stuff is what has infected the nation's finances. These little red areas are where Tea Party members of Congress call home.

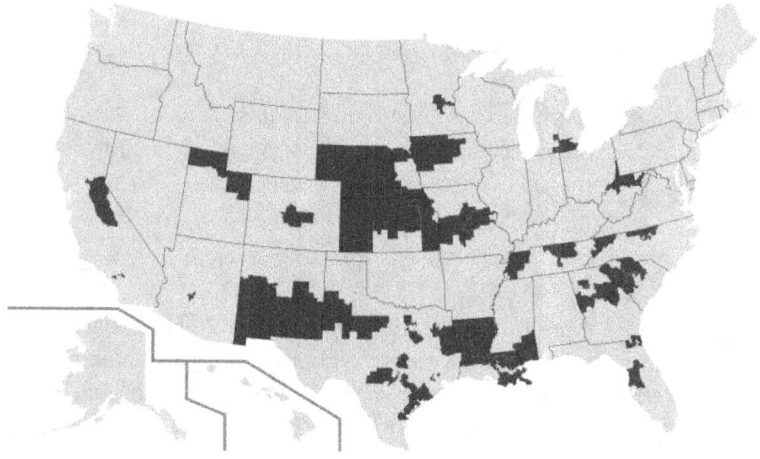

This isn't exactly a nice cross section of the nation. Literally, these red areas decided how best to run the WHOLE entire country.

Heck, those Mormons in Utah have a hard time managing all their wives — who are they to decide the fate of the rest of the nation.

A casual glance at the chart demonstrates that the areas are back-waters, folksy and given to anti-guv-mint hallucinations. I should know I was born in a back-waters village in Michigan and lived in Bastrop Texas. I know my back-waters stomping grounds!

I can also see why Michele Bachmann is the 'receptacle' of this Tea Party Caucus movement. She speaks in **Absolutes** about issues she doesn't understand. Ignorance is its own battle-cry for these people. They don't want to be right. They just want to win. Michele's rational for causing a Federal shutdown? In her own words:

"I think the reason is because President Obama can't wait to get Americans addicted to the crack cocaine of dependency on more government health care. Because, once they enroll millions of more individual Americans it will be virtually impossible for us to pull these benefits back from people."

Really? Health care is not 'crack cocaine' for the masses. Do you really think a 4 year old with an asthma attack is 'addicted' to the crack cocaine of health care? Perhaps the little kid just wants to live. Perhaps his parents want her to live.

Perhaps America is big enough that we ALL want a little kid to survive a night of deathly illness. Perhaps we want to protect society from contagious outbreaks for the safety of the nation. However, to accomplish this rather modest goal of public safety, we need parents to take sick kids for medical care instead of sending them to school because they fear the costs will destroy the family.

● ● ● ●

In fact, ACA might actually succeed if given an honest chance and some good oversight. The future is never certain on brand new laws. However, what is certain is that a government can't give services to citizens if the doors are closed due to a shutdown. Existing laws that work become defunct when unfunded.

To Grover Norquist and his crew, blackmail is the only solution. This LAW doesn't satisfy these elitist (rich... did I mention rich?) pirates, so they seize the nation by the throat.

But, First-Mate Bachmann is not alone on the hijacking. She has other bright lights celebrating her narrow point of view. How about this answer when asked if it's okay for the nation to go into default at the hands of the Tea Party Caucus blackmailers:

> *"We don't know, we haven't ever done it," Rep. Steve Stockman, R-Texas, told ABC News, when asked what happens when the nation defaults.*

Well, I've never cut off my thumbs before either — but I'm pretty sure it's a bad idea.

These legislators are so clueless to reality they don't understand running the nation requires both cash, and a functional government.

Even that fundamental concept cannot find root in the dust-bowl of their synapses.

● ● ● ●

So, let me talk about a specific sticking point for these extortionists.

The problem isn't the debt. They had this debt problem since 1979.

The sticking point really is giving citizens 'health care benefits'.

To deny these benefits, they seize the government and immediately, deceased veterans can't get the dignity of proper burials. They seize the government and kids are denied cancer treatment.

They seize the government without knowing or CARING about the repercussions.

They say the battleground is the Affordable Health Care Act.

The argument goes that healthcare is not a '*right*' but a '*responsibility*' of an individual.

The argument further goes that '*responsibilities*' aren't the prevue of the government.

Therefore, ergo-facto, the Act (which is a law) must be overthrown via extortion — and Americans everywhere should kiss the rings upon these 49 legislators' fingers.

Well… except these Tea Party Legislators get much better care then 95% of the nation. Some people will live like royalty.

● ● ● ●

Let me tell you a story.

Imagine you drive out of the city. Less than 10 miles out there is no electricity. That means no gas stations. That means no medical care.

Heck, for these Tea Party faithful, that means no Wal-Marts in corn fields.

Just darkness as you drive out of the cities.

Well, 90 years ago that was the case in America. Just darkness

The social program then under siege by the grandfathers of these idiots was 'rural electrification'.

In order to fight ol' timey Tea Party "*no electricity on my watch*" politic-granpappy, here is what good-guy Morris L. Cooke had to say in 1935 about putting up power poles beyond city limits to:

> *"Farms are factories as well as homes; therefore the electrification of rural America means more than comfort and convenience. It means profit to farmer, to utility, to appliance manufacturer."*

14

In the face of the benefits of electricity, a small fraction of bigoted politicians felt that rural America did not deserve electricity because rural America could not AFFORD to build electricity for itself.

The rural electrification program was fought tooth and nail by those fat-cat politicians who felt it was a guv-mint handout.

Please note, those politician were correct in a few important details:

1. the farmers could not build power plants
2. the farmers could not run wires
3. the farmers could not PAY for the infrastructure in the slightest.

This was all true.

However, what would have happened if America had listened and NOT PUT POWER into rural settings?

Well, we would not be America. The Nazis would have kicked our asses. If not the Nazis – then the Japanese and Nazis together – would have kicked our asses. You see, America was able to fight after Pearl Harbor because the *gov-mint,* social program handed-out power to everybody — a true 'crack cocaine of dependency' in 1935. Only this crack was electrical crack, and those dirty rural addicts burned it up like it was energy or something.

So, who was right? The rich power companies that wanted to keep farmers poor, and in the dark; or the visionaries that believe America was better with coast to coast electricity?

EVERY COMPLEX PROBLEM HAS AN EASY TO UNDERSTAND WRONG ANSWER.

● ● ● ●

Our nation is what it is today because smarter people recognized the VALUE in equality for all Americans. Smart people stood up to dumb people, and made electricity happen.

In our modern hour we have the same dumb people — but the smart people are acting like enormous wimps.

These new pirates only want power for themselves. In fact, these Tea Party idiots even resent F.D. Roosevelt's program of rural electrification.

Imagine, driving out of the city into nothing but darkness. No gas stations, no restaurants, no emergency services, no lights on highways – in fact – no highways at all.

Notice how similar the political resistance is between Rural Electrification in 1935 and Affordable Care Act of 2013. Here's a synopsis of the resistance to electricity from the Tennessee Valley Authority Website:

In the 1930s, nearly 90 percent of urban dwellers had electricity, compared to only 10 percent of rural dwellers. Private utility companies, which supplied electric power to most of the nation's consumers, argued that it was too expensive to string electric lines to isolated rural farmsteads. In addition, they argued that most farmers were too poor to afford electricity.

Rural electrification was based on the belief that affordable electricity would improve the standard of living and the economic competitiveness of the family farm. The Roosevelt Administration believed that if private enterprise could not supply electric power to the people, then it was the duty of the government to do it.

Most of the court cases involving the TVA during the 1930s concerned the government's involvement in the public utilities industry. By 1941, the TVA had become the largest producer of electrical power in the United States. That led to strong opposition from power companies, who were angered by the cheaper energy available through TVA, and saw it as a threat to private development.

They charged that the federal government's involvement in the power business was unconstitutional. During the 1930s, numerous court challenges were brought against the TVA. In the end, the Supreme Court ruled that the TVA had the authority to generate power, to sell the electricity, and to distribute that electricity.

Additionally, the TVA set up the Electric Home and Farm Authority to help farmers purchase major electric appliances. The EHFA made arrangements with appliance makers to supply electric ranges, refrigerators and water heaters at affordable prices, which were then sold at local power companies and electric cooperatives. A farmer could purchase appliances there with loans offered by the EHFA, which offered low-cost financing.

Source: http://www.u-s-history.com/pages/h1653.html

Neo-Cons both Old and New

1935: Electricity BAAAAAADD!
2013: Health Care BAAAAAADD!

America without Electricity? If those old-timey neo-cons succeeded back in 1935 then the course of Human History would have tipped into the hands of Military dictatorship.

America would be like North Korea is right now. Dark.

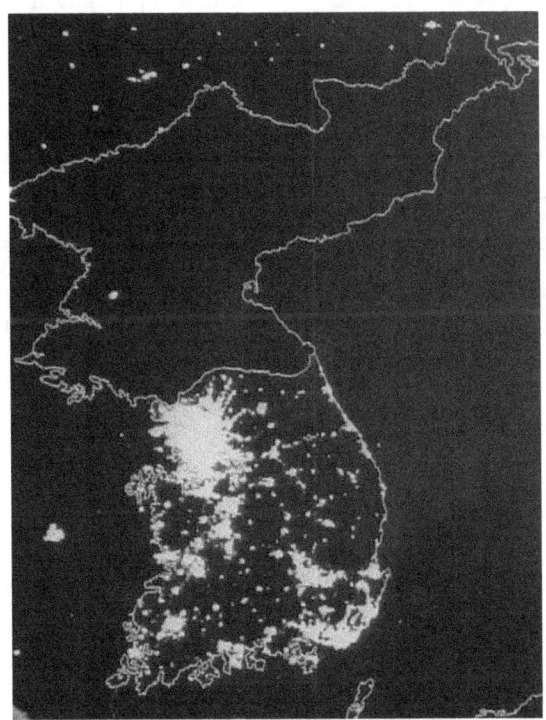

Picture: Scientific American. North Korea at night.

These Tea Party Caucus politicians are not democratic leaders, but brazen anarchist who wants to be KINGS over the masses.

Make no mistake, these simpletons are evil. Not in a Darth Vader kind of evil...because he ultimately turned from the dark side. But in an over-zealous, rabid ideologue kind of evil.

It is truly evil tyranny when a small cliché feels so superior over others they seize freedom by extortion.

● ● ● ●

So as a humorist, I made a point of lampooning the ignorance of Michele Bachmann's crew of tyrants. But, there is much more at stake than just some laughs.

I am not a conspiracy theorist. I don't believe it takes a super-villain to mess something up. In this case, it only takes ignorant superiority to push the nation into shutdown.

However, Michele Bachmann doesn't have the strength, intellect, nor charisma to cause this crisis by herself. It does take a leader. Not a super-villain leader, but just a self-absorbed idealist who is mean enough to bully the nation around.

Power for Michele Bachmann comes from a single lobbyist:

GROVER NORQUIST

The United States of America effectively stopped functioning at the will of a single, psychopath's will.

It is no mistake to say that all this comes from a single origin.

Shutting down the government is the wrong answer.

Our wrong answer is Grover Norquist.

Shutting down Grover Norquist and the Tea Party Caucus is the right answer.

● ● ● ●

A Nation Shutters Its Doors

CHAPTER 2

The Little Dictator of Democracy

Did you know that a single gram of salt kills a rat? It's true. Everything is a poison when misused, over concentrated, and put into the wrong system.

Lobbyists are salt...er...if politics are rats. Ah, forget it. My analogy got too messy from the first sentence. Just like politics, rats and salt.

Grover Norquist is one of those things that might be healthy if restricted to a smattering here and there. However, he is the main ingredient in the Republican soup. Norquist is a chubby little guy too, so that's a really salty soup with his pudgy body floating around in the mix.

Norquist is a lobbyist. That's it. Just a lobbyist.

Not just any kind lobbyist though. Grover Norquist is first and foremost, a lobbyist for the uber-rich. This scientific taxonomy of this particular breed of lobbyist is called a *"lobbyrichguyus prickus"*. The most lethal of all the lobbyist species.

He is shrewd. Don't let my satire make you think I am lampooning a feeble-brained ideologue. Grover is smart enough to dress up his lobbyist ideals in wonderful sounding mantles. Mantles of words that charm the innocent of heart. For example:

"**Americans For Tax Reform**" — which is simply a patriotic sounding lobby to give the super-rich a ZERO tax rate. Oh, and also not allow any help for the elderly — because as Norquist says, "The only thing the government should do for the elderly is get out of their way." I guess dear old granny who can't drive, or walk, should skip her Meals-On-Wheels program. Norquist's perspective is that the government should get out of granny's way so she can just die already, and reduce the surplus population of Social Security using elder-thugs.

In Norquist's defense, it is obvious that "*Americans For Tax Reform*" sounds better than "*Bless The Rich, Screw the Middle Class, Loath The Poor*". The second name would be the proper title if Lobbies were named after what they truly did. However, lobbyists like Grover generally don't like tipping their hands with honesty. It's hard for them to get what their little egotistical hearts want if the world is open and honest.

"**Alliance For Worker Freedom**" — This one AMAZES me. The AFWF true purpose is to remove all worker rights to wage and benefit negotiation. Well, this flies in the face of the rugged American individualism that Norquist supposedly embraces. He wants to keep workers from being so rugged that they dare negotiate their own wages. Grover claims the ethos of free-will is his inner core. Maybe he even believes himself — but he doesn't extend free-will to honest workers. Great liars are all self-deluded. Norquist is a great liar.

What the Alliance for Worker Freedom does is violate citizens Constitutional Right to negotiate fair wages. Per Grover, workers are supposed to beg for their daily bread from the always magnanimous and fair hands of their benevolent masters. AFWF is a fraud. Why would Grover Norquist even start such an organization?

The only explanation could be if BUSINESS plutocrats are actually underwriting the costs of this 'worker freedom' program, in order to force slave-labor in order to maximize corporate gain. V.I. Lenin would be proud of Norquist's usage of propaganda. Not a single word is honest in "Alliance for Worker Freedom". Not alliance. Not Workers. Not Free. Even the word "For" is highly suspect in this bit of propaganda. Its actual title should be **Masters Subjugating Feudal Serfs** (MSFS) which would certainly sound delightfully nostalgic to Norquist.

The Ronald Reagan Occult... er... I mean "**The Ronald Reagan Legacy Project**" (RRLP). Norquist wants to put a Ronald

Reagan statue in EVERY single county in the nation. No joke. I'm not being a humorist at all at the moment. The RRLP is a real thing.

That goal is to put a Reagan Memorial (altar? temple? Crèche?) in every county in America. Quoth Mr. Norquist:

> **"In addition to ensuring that every February 6th is known as "Ronald Reagan Day," we work to encourage the naming of landmarks, buildings, roads, etc. after Ronald Wilson Reagan. ... Each one of these dedications serve as a teaching moment for those who were not yet alive during his presidency .... Our goal is to eventually see a statue, park, or road named after Reagan in all the counties in the United States."**

I like Reagan — perhaps everybody but Air Traffic Controllers likes Reagan — but do I have to worship him? Can't I just like him? Must my like be turned into zealous worship?

I don't even think Ronald Reagan would want this kind of gratuitous idol-worship. In true megalomaniac verve, the cult, I mean RRLP, doesn't want to stop at putting up Reagan altars in America. Like any good cult leader, Norquist latches onto the charismatic icon of Reagan, reflects that image back onto himself, and spreads the new gospel around the globe. Norquist makes himself the Muhammad of Allah, The Joseph Smith of Mormonism, the personal representative of famous President Reagan.

By being Reagan's most ardent fan, Grover Norquist steals Reagan's mantle. It is theft by appropriation.

Also, have you thought about how many counties there are in America? A ton right? Let me Google that, brb....

I found, via deep research and thousands of hours of study, that Wiki says there are 3,033 counties in America. (BTW, Wiki is the satirists' favorite reference. Writing political humor is like Wikipedia, horse-shoes and hand-grenades; close enough is perfect. I digress).

Hey, did you notice I used two Internet abbreviations (brb & btw) in the paragraph above? I'm hip like that. LOL. Not only am I Internet hip, I'm also pragmatically smart.

If there are 3,033 counties in America that means Grover Norquist will need A LOT of time and money. What sounds like a noble goal is, in fact, just a con to install Grover as the Reagan mouthpiece until the day Norquist dies.

Grover Norquist is *STEALING* Ronald Reagan's mystique.

BTW. LOL. LMFAO. Grover Norquist says there are 3,140 counties. I don't know who to believe anymore. Wiki or Norquist? At any rate, Norquist wants even _more_ than I original researched. Ah, to be an ego-maniacal maniac. There are no limits.

The *Ronald Reagan Legacy Project* is a con.

A shakedown. The RRLP soils the name of a famous President, with the petulant fingers of a mere lobbyist. Ah, it is the essence of today's politics. A pungent aroma of rotting false-pretenses that makes our eyes water with the tears of noxious patriotism.

Sniff... Reagan... *sniff...* statues... America... Norquist... *sniff.*

However, it is actually just Grover manure piled up in a corner. Our eyes water because the vapors are so strong.

Newsflash My late breaking research says the goal of the RRLP is not just American counties. It is the world! The whole entire fricken' world. Behold! The Norquist ConQuist! (*Conquest* + '*Norquist*' makes a new word! Behold the '*Con-Quist*' of freedom and liberty. ConQuist. Use it today! TM and Copyright Stephen Paul West. All rights reserved. Tiny words, fast talk.

So, Norquist wants to install Ronald Reagan statues around the world, but especially in Communist countries. You know, for a guy who claims to believe in citizens directing their own destiny, this is definitely the opposite of citizenry free-will. Instead, he jams Reagan down people's throats like a Mormon Missionary latching onto a recent widow with a broken front porch rail.

Seriously, I know that Ronald Reagan would not approve of this. Isn't a statue project EXACTLY like Stalin, Lenin, Pol Pot, Mao

Tse-Tung, Hitler and every other despot in history who MUST proclaim themselves deity among humanity?

Statues all over the world doesn't sound like the Gipper does it?

I am sure Grover is co-opting Reagan's identity to co-opt the Republican Party. Grover gets to be the Moses of Mount Reagan to the GOP faithful. (Admittedly, another analogy of mine that has run amok. However, I don't have time to remove the extra prose. I'm on a deadline.)

Reagan was a rather humble man in behavior. He didn't wear flannel shirts and split his own wood for good PR. Unlike today's politicians who must up-spin every-single-thing they do that sounds work-y class-y; Reagan actually did split wood and wear flannel just because he liked it. Good president.

Just like George Washington, however, Reagan would also refuse to be made King. Especially, posthumously by a pompous twit like Norquist; a self-serving Jester Who Would Be King.

Norquist is not the personal emissary of Reagan.

Norquist is the *"Jester Who Would Be King"*.

How did this happen? Did he invent a super-mind control raygun?

Sadly, he blinded the GOP with the image of Reagan and then used words little enough that the Republicans believed the simple-minded message of Grover Norquist.

Grover Norquist is a fascist who is running a '*lobbitary coup*' to overthrow our government. This is much less bloody than your typical '*military coup*' but the end result is still a government removed from the hands of citizenry.

(See what I did there? Lobbitary Coup! I combined '*military coup*' + '*lobbist*' to create a brand new word. This is what comedy writers do best; make up stuff. However, if this one word gets into the dictionary my entire existence is justified! I would become IMMORTAL. My ego is no less than Grover Norquist's! Just I didn't start with uber-rich parents, and I'm not in politics. Still, I shall rule them all!)

Charles Taylor and Grover Norquist must have instant chat. They both understand how to destroy a nation using proxy warlords and simple sounding demagoguery.

'Lobbitary Coup'. Use it today! TM and Copyright Stephen Paul West. All rights reserved. Tiny words, fast talk.

> "In today's news the United States of America was overthrown in a Lobbitary Coup. Details at eleven."

How does one simply walk into Mordor? How does a tiny hobbit like Norquist simply take over the government?

27

It is the pledge of power, which I shall analyze quite thoroughly later.

Unlike J.R. Tolkien's symbol of evil bondage, there is not a golden ring of power. Norquist uses a little piece of paper, and about 275 Republican Ninnies who trade the pledge of office to a pledge to "The Pledge." (*queue the sinister Druid music chanting in the background*).

However, inside those 275 regular Norquist Republics there lurks a darker lot — The Tea Party Caucus.

They are the 49 who shut down the nation. They are so stubborn they won't even listen the regular Republicans that sold out to Norquist and his evil pledge.

Norquist's Pledge (*queue sinister Druid chant*).

It is the evil that binds them all. It rules them all.

> In the Land of Norquist where the Shadows lie.
> One Pledge to rule them all, One Pledge to find them,
> One Pledge to bring them all and in the darkness bind them.
> In the Land of Norquist where the Shadows lie.
> And jack-diddly gets done in Congress.
>
> — *J.R.R. Tolkien, The Lord of the Rings (more or less)*

Understanding Norquist, and The Pledge that binds them, requires I slip the constraints of mortality.

First, I must put the reader into a time machine and go back to when America was perfect. Back to a time when Nixon was President. Back to a time before the GOVERNMENT ruined everything with taxes and social programs.

Back to the imaginary past so heart-fully believed to exist by Norquist's peons; the Tea Party and GOP of Norquist.

The time when America had no problems. (No problems except for those pesky minorities, women, Korean War, Vietnam War, The Cold War and Nuclear proliferation. But those aren't really the *real* America of Norquist's legions of ignorant flying monkeys.)

Hey, I just combined LOTR movie references with the Wizard of Oz! I am so amazing, I amaze myself. Soon, I shall be as egotistically splendid as Grover.

The day is October 19, 1956. Baby Grover Glenn Norquist is born.

Close your eyes and embrace the lie... back... reject the truth... back... you are slipping the bonds of reality... back... back... there are no social programs of any kind... back... no social security... no government roads... back... no rural electrification... no welfare... no sin... no uppity women... back... no minorities anywhere... close your eyes and reject reality... feel the heart of Norquist...

BIRTH!

CHAPTER 3

Behold! Ayn Rand Is In ~~Labor~~!

(Actually, she hates labor)

• • • •

You have arrived. You are witnessing the birth of Grover Norquist. October 19, 1956

Ayn Rand is squirming on the cold, stainless steel bed. She likes the dead feeling stimulating her spine. She refuses to allow the doctors to call it 'labor' however. She hates that looter and moocher class of working serfs. Not labor. No! She wants this birthing process to be called; "Passing Through Dagny's Valley"

Suddenly, a baby is born!

A pudgy little face.

Ten perfect toes. Ten perfect fingers.

And no heart…

The baby immediately slaps Ayn Rand to demonstrate that offering help just makes people dependent upon each other. Ewww. Who would want that? If this baby accepts any care, it will lead to a life of idle, welfare loafing.

● ● ● ●

BTW – I am really sorry to anybody born after 1984 who reads this satire. Unfortunately, most of the key components of what's crippling America at this moment come from historical opinions rendered by zealot-nuts way back in the 1950's.

● ● ● ●

Ayn Rand weeps a moment as she has the episiotomy stitched on her Galt's Gulch. She lets this unnamed, heartless baby suck the uncaring Kool-Aid of her cold breasts.

And then, she walks out on the infant. She knows he will be better making his own way in the world rather than accept any handouts.

The baby draws a breath to cry out, and it boldly proclaims;

"Run for your life from any man who tells you that money is evil. That sentence is the leper's bell of an approaching moocher."

Is this heartless baby without hope? No, Ayn Rand was right! Handouts just make people weak. It forces the redistribution of wealth from the productive parent-class to that needy, begging, infant-class.

Communism at its worse.

So our heartless, unnamed baby, walks strongly out of the hospital and crossing the street, marches boldly up the stairs to the Headquarters of Polaroid Corporation.

Yes, the heartless baby could choose a lowly janitor for a parent – but no – that is morally wrong. As wrong as being born into poverty, or being old and needing help with medical needs. The government is evil. Personal self-will is the ONLY solution.

Fortunately, the vitriol-milk from Ayn Rand's breast is perfect sustenance for the heartless. The unknown baby whips his umbilical cord around like Indiana Jones snapping a whip. *Pow*! The baby hits elevator button to the Penthouse suite! Just as it planned.

The heartless baby strolls into the Vice President of Polaroid Office, and negotiates a business deal, whereby said baby will deliver the world from all government control in exchange for Vice Presidents everywhere not having to pay a fricken' cent in taxes!

Behold the birth of our Grover! Our baby Grover Norquist shows just how every person on earth should be totally self-directed and absolutely independent of any assistance.

Ayn Rand is proud. The identity of the father has forever been hotly speculated. The most promising candidates are Sam Walton, Donald Trump or the Tin-Man; as all of these men lived without any heart.

● ● ● ●

I will admit this 1950's hero-worship problem was exactly why I had to resort to the *deus ex machina* of time travel earlier. Shakespeare would be furious at my sleight-of-hand. Still, how else can I explain the dogmatic fixation of listening to Grover Norquist? I need time travel to even begin to explain the current idiocracy in American politics (woot! Another movie reference).

I cannot, for the life of me explain, even by using satire, why modern America has become stabbed to death by the failed ideology of the 1950's.

I think my story of Norquist's birth makes just about as much sense as anything else.

● ● ● ●

So, the baby and Vice President of Polaroid complete the clean, sterile, important matters of business. Now comes a stupid human part. The infant must be named.

"Grover" as in "Grover Cleveland" both the 22nd and the 24th President of the United States.

Now, President Grover Cleveland had a real personal vision. That vision was *SUPER CONSERVATIVISM*. Strangely, he was the candidate of the Democrat party. (I find it so weird that the Democrats used to be the Republicans once upon a time. Weirder still is to think about Abe Lincoln. Lincoln was Republican. What? The Republicans of Lincoln's day were more like the Democrats of today. How many times have these two parties crossed-dressed in each other clothing?)

At any rate, there was nothing wrong with President Grover Cleveland's personal ethics.

The problem was his too narrow and controlling view of how to **run** the nation.

President Grover Cleveland actually **ruined** the nation.

The only difference between 'run' and 'ruin' is the 'i' — as in I wish Lobbyist Grover Norquist would leave the country alone already. This was the same wish many hungry Americans muttered in the late 1890s. When Grover Cleveland was beating the suffing out of the country with his uber-conservative policies.

However, Grover was selected as a name for the heartless baby. And, like a curse, the name choice doomed the child Norquist to the same fate (but lacking the integrity and strength of President Cleveland, our Grover Norquist just became a maggoty lobbyist. The bane of modern American freedom). To paraphrase a great historian about Grover (either one of them, past or present):

> Grover opposed high tariffs, Free Silver*, inflation, imperialism and subsidies to business, farmers or veterans. His battles for political reform and fiscal conservatism made him <u>an icon for American conservatives</u> of the era. **Disaster hit the nation as his second term began when the Panic of 1893 produced a severe national depression that Grover Cleveland was unable to reverse**. It ruined his Democratic party**
>
> President Cleveland took strong positions [to break unions] and was heavily criticized. His intervention in the Pullman Strike of 1894 to keep the railroads moving angered labor unions nationwide and angered the party in Illinois; his support of the gold standard and opposition to Free Silver alienated the agrarian wing of the Democratic Party.
>
> Furthermore, critics complained that he had <u>little imagination</u> and seemed overwhelmed by the nation's economic disasters – depressions and strikes – in his second term. – *The esteemed Mr. Wi K. Pedia (more or less)*

Free Silver Policy would have redistributed wealth from the uber-rich Gold owners, to the working class who could only afford the lesser silver. Grover Cleveland opposed this fair redistribution, and felt farmers should worry about 'their toil and not their wealth'.

**I know it's so weird that extreme conservatives USED to be the Democrats. This policy destroyed the Democrat* *party for decades after Cleveland. Tee hee! Funny! I betcha the GOP is already getting their helping of Grover Hyper-Conservative ruin even as I type. American is voting out the neo-cons.*

The voting public can only be tricked by bad policies for so long before they finally figure out the snake that bit them — and they cut off the serpent's head with a sharpened hoe.

Woe! Woe! Unto those neo-conservatives who do not learn their history! For they are DOOOMED to repeat the past.

President Grover Cleveland's opposition to taxes and anti-labor stance, coupled with his strong faith in the super-rich to fix the economy <u>destroyed</u> the nation for twenty years.

Lobbyist Grover Norquist's opposition to taxes and labor, coupled with his strong opinion that the rich will fix the economy has <u>destroyed</u> this nation for the last twenty years.

The exact same policies of two Grovers, a full century apart, will result in TWO depressions for the exact same reasons. Make no mistake Grover Norquist really does want to ru(i)n the nation.

> **"Yes. I want to stand on the side lines and clap my hands. When the citizens do my will."***

*an actual quote of the adult Grover Norquist.

It's sad. It's sad because America really will suffer. I'm stepping out of the satirist role a moment, to teach a little lesson of truth. America has a right to thrive, and that only comes with moderate policies, proper regulations of the super-wealthy and super-powerful, and a faith in labor and unions.

Back to being the humor! Woot!

Grover Norquist became doomed to repeat the mistakes of his namesake, President Grover Cleveland. However, our modern Grover lacks any of President Cleveland's redeeming qualities, like honesty and personal character — and most importantly an <u>elected</u> office.

However, Norquist does have the 'lack of imagination' part of the previous president, down to a science.

● ● ● ●

I think I should point out once again. Grover Norquist is JUST a lobbyist.

Only a lobbyist.

His influence should never create the party policies of the Republicans. Grover Norquist is not an elected official, unlike President Grover Cleveland.

President Grover Cleveland earned, by the right of the vote, for his policies to ruin the nation.

Lobbyist Grover Norquist is just a bully, hack and despot who managed to hijack 95% of the Republican Party, and thus paralyze everything in the Congress and Senate.

Grover Norquist never got a single vote from a single citizen—ever.

Why is Norquist making public policy then?

Only because the GOP can't stand up to a school yard bully. And this brings me to Grover Norquist's childhood!

● ● ● ●

CHILDHOOD OF EVIL

CHAPTER 4

Getting all the ideas needed by the ripe old age of 12.

"The Taxpayer Protection Pledge was something I came up with when I was twelve years old. I wrote it in 1968 when I was in seventh grade. At twelve some things are simple." – Grover Norquist at the Age of 56.

It is honestly true that Grover Norquist's pledge is based on his idea of taxation at the age of twelve.

Twelve years old?

What could a kid, raised in extreme wealth, know about taxation?

Maybe he threw a tantrum when the maid took away the scissors he was using to snip the ears off a commie, needy, puppy? That maid's bureaucratic seizure of his *'scissor rights'* forever made him hate taxation and the working class.

At any rate, this nation is being ripped apart by the document of a twelve year old from 1968.

Pathetic is that the Republican Party accepts this pre-pubescent ideology as modern, irrevocable and permanent doctrine. This ardent fixation of a child's manifesto is destroying the nation. This may explain why Repubs are willing to block, filibuster and deny anything except their OWN selfish ideals. They are exactly like petulant, rich, egomaniacal, selfish children. The Norquist Pledge has infected their brains with infantile syndrome.

Have you noticed that I have not actually shown you the image of the sacred Norquist Pledge. I'm trying to build up suspense. I will show you later in a very special chapter. So, pour a bowl of cereal and don't touch that dial. The Thunder-Cats will be back in a flash! Retro Alert! Retro Alert! I should select a show from 1968, but I have no fricken idea what existed back before the world had colors. BRB. Google Time... let's see... A proper show would have been Mayberry RFD; and perhaps this show influenced Grover Norquist into believing the nation is a fictional backwater's town with silly characters and tiny needs.

Twelve-year-olds should NOT be deciding the nation.

Twelve-year-olds certainly do NOT understand taxation and managing something as complex as the U.S. of A.

Especially, twelve year olds who live a privileged life.

Maybe I would trust the Little Rascals, or little orphan Annie to know something about supply and demand. Those kids had the crap kicked out of them, and understood the value of money and the necessity of helping the unfortunate.

Grover Norquist was the son of a wealthy Vice President of a Fortune 100 company. His family was LlooOOAAAaaaDdded!

So, this rich, over-privileged, over-indulged, child figured out how to run a nation?

As a bonus he decided this in 1968, from the cold security of his all white, gated community.

And we are ALL stuck with the mandate of a twelve-year-old from 1968.

Or, NOT.

How about the Republicans grow a pair and stand up to a twelve year old bully? If they all reject The Pledge then little-boy Grover

Norquist will be vanquished. He will not be able to bully them, coerce elections via money, and attack Repubs in a focused hate.

• • • •

The problem is that Neo-Cons love overly simplistic solutions. They actually '*get*' what twelve year olds are saying.

Shocking! How can I make such a brash and ridiculous statement! Bolderdash! I should be ashamed....

Two words in my defense: Jonathan Krohn

Maybe you have forgotten the GOPs' worship of the previous Twelve Year Old Prophet of Neo-Con-ism.

He was little Jonathan Krohn.

And how the neo-cons loved him – and his deep thoughts.

This Jonathan Krohn was the hero of Neo-Cons at the ripe old age of 13. Thirteen! Are you fricken' kidding me? Did he even have a job? Answer: No.

Cute kid, though. The point is that he is a kid, though.

• • • •

However, the above pre-pubescent Jonathan Krohn wrote the book "*Defining Conservatism*" and addressed the Conservative Political Action Conference at age 14. Krohn used his 'life' savings to self-publish his book and explained hardcore core conservative principles through the lens of a 14 year old boy.

And the Neo-Con understood his immature words.

And embraced them to heart.

Neo-Cons, such as Grover Norquist, understood a boy but are scared by the complexity of a world they cannot control nor comprehend. So, they made a 14 year old King of their religion. CNN and the Fox News interviewed the boy repeatedly. His second book, "*Defining Conservatism: The Principles That Will Bring Our*

Country Back," garnered just as much sycophantic accolades as the first book. Mind you, these are not dragon books of fiction. These are complete taxation and socio-economic thesis statements, er... written by a 14 year old. Certainly, every word must be truth.

But, by the Age of 17, the Jonathan Krohn shown below, rejected neo-conservatism and openly states he is... wait for it... wait for it... a LIBERAL.

And CNN and Fox News have not interviewed the more mature Krohn since.

Jonathan Krohn certainly deserves the right to grow, mature and change his world view as he learns more about the world. This Jonathan Krohn has a more compassionate and functional world view:

Notice the liberal Jonathan Krohn has facial hair?

I propose the Neo-Cons only accept doctrine from folks that have at least a strand or two of body hair. Just sayin'

However, fundamentalist can't handle complexity. They must have very small, simple-to-understand answers; even if those answers are wrong. Obviously, in a complex situation a simplistic view is childish, unformed and, therefore, incorrect.

And this is why Norquist's Pledge — based on his vision as a twelve-year-old, spoiled, child — has captured the hearts of neo-con, fundamentalists, Tea Party Members and Republicanites everywhere. They get it. It feels safe. It is a sound bite against the swirling noise of the world.

Tiny. Small. Easy to digest. A safe little blurb in the face of a broad and teeming world.

Norquist offers a little floatie in a three foot swimming pool.

But, the world offers the ocean. Norquist can't manage reality.

In fact, most of the beauty in this world is caused by randomness, and a huge cosmos beyond human control.

Grover Norquist never matured. He didn't have too. His life was one of endless privilege and this has turned him into the *Peter Pan* of politics.

The GOP plays the part of *The Lost Boys*. Unfortunately, the uber-conservatives don't have any women as clever and sexy as *Tinker Bell*. Sarah Palin and Michele Bachmann? Pshssspt! The Tea Party does have a tons of Pirates! The Jack Abramoffs of the world love Grover Norquist and his immature mind. The Pirates manipulate him as easily as taking candy from a baby.

I hate it when Grover Norquist claps his little hands together on TV. I'll admit that my stomach lurches at the pitter-patter of Grover's hands. Why must he clap like a pre-pubescent boy? He is fifty-six. Grover Norquist, at the age of FIFTY-SIX, used the word "Poopy-head" on national television.

The guy who is responsible for the partisan gridlock, unfinanced debt and GOP double-down on a bad policy, is also the guy who uses baby talk to explain his concept of national elections.

He thus proved my point that he is a selfish wee-boy trapped in a pudgy, double-chinned body. Poopy Head. Really? Really?

So, Grover Norquist is proud he has not matured beyond a twelve year old. He is proud he wrote his Pledge at twelve, and that he stuck to his guns. He is proud he has doubled-down on his bad bet that he made when he didn't even have distended testicles.

What about Jonathan Krohn, the young boy who matured into a new idea? Maybe someday Jonathan will change his mind again. Who knows?

However, let's hear from a more mature, ex-conservative, ex-GOP, ex-Grover Norquist golden child — Jonathan Krohn:

> "What does a kid who has never paid a tax bring to the table in a conversation about the burden of taxes? What does a healthy child know about people who can't afford healthcare because of preexisting conditions? No matter how intelligent a person might be, certain political issues require life experience; they're much more complicated than the black and white frames imposed by partisan America
>
> I have been treated by the political right with all the maturity of schoolyard bullies. The Daily Caller, for instance, wrote three articles about my shift, topping it off with an opinion piece in which they stated that I deserved criticism because I wear "thick-rimmed glasses" and I like Ludwig Wittgenstein. Why don't they just call me "four-eyes"?
>
> These are not adults leveling serious criticism; these are scorned right-wingers showing all the maturity of a little boy.
>
> No wonder I fit in so well when I was 13."

Jonathan Krohn changed.

So can the nation.

Grover Norquist is stuck with the adolescent brain of a twelve year old.

Meanwhile the nation is stuck in a spiral of noxious resistance and crazy, immature politics, because of a temper-tantrum of this lobbyist.

COLLEGE YEARS

CHAPTER 5

Yeah Nixon! And a little bit of cross dressing too!

Harvard! That's right, you worm infested stinkards of the middle class. Harvard!

You cannot even dare to smell the campus of Harvard while driving past in your late-model, practical cars.

Furthermore, you poor shall not even have the teeth, nor food to even utter the word, "*Harvard.*" For it is a sacred word. No '*free gift*' of health-care, or government cheese for you ugly poor. If you all had just gone to Harvard you wouldn't be mooching and looting. You poor made a terrible choice and deserve no cake.

For Harvard is the alma mater of one, Grover Glenn Norquist.

Certainly, he learned a lot about life in such an elitist, hallowed, campus. I'm glad he is defining the best policies for the poor, hungry, sick, vulnerable and even the middle class in this nation. His experience in those areas is zero. So, why not?

There can't be a single problem with a Harvard Graduate from a privilege childhood defining the social programs of America.

Hey! We all remember college life, right?

Cramming for exams. The occasional party. Sometimes staying out late. Running around with our friends. Being wild and carefree!

Man it felt great!

We all joined that rad club called "*College Republican National Committee*" and did that insane door to door canvassing for Richard Nixon to be elected President.

Am I Right? Am I Right?

Richard Nixon and Vietnam. Two great tastes that taste great together. Norquist was so turned on by Nixon that he had this to say:

"I was one of the guys who helped staff [Richard Nixon's Fundraiser], as a volunteer, and they said,

'Oh, you're not going to be able to go because your hair's too long.'

I always had long hair and thought that Janis Joplin was the high point of Western civilization. I never saw any conflict in that and being for liberty. I always thought they were sort of the same thing.

The [Nixon] party people backed off, but that was a brief hiccup in my participation in American politics."

What a blast! I mean, wow, the expression on the Nation's face when Watergate hit! Vietnam! Yeah-hah!

A defiant, long haired Norquist taking on the Nixon people, so he could arrange a fund-raiser. *Whew!*

Of course, it was those stinkard poor and middle class that Norquist watched go fight and die in rice paddies while Grover stayed safely behind Harvard's Ivy covered walls. The war was almost over after 19 years, 5 months, 4 weeks, 1 day; but if you remember I gave you Grover's birthday. Yes, Grover Norquist turned 18 just in time that he COULD have joined the war and fought for a half year of good times.

Young Norquist opted out of Vietnam and instead even got to play President of his *College Republican National Committee.* These young

College Repubs doggedly preached in favor of American fighting endlessly in a protracted war (does any of this sound like déjà vu' or is it just me?) These were the same young, rich, spoiled pricks who refused to join and fight besides the boys who were drafted.

Before his death, the architect of the Vietnam war, Robert McNamara, made a confession that he regretted engineering the Vietnam war. At age 93, the designer of the Vietnam War became the most ardent opponent against the Iraq War. These pointless wars piled on debt and spending without any thought by the Tea Party Caucus. It will take 100 years to pay off the two recent wars. And every Tea Party Caucus member supported the waste.

We all know that Mitt Romney was just empty money. No wonder he wanted – literally – an endless war. Think of all the money those underpaid troops will make for CEO's everywhere.

> "Killing is the business. And business is good."
> – *Major Payne and Grover Norquist*

I do not know if Robert McNamara redeemed himself. For certain, his rebuke against the Iraq and Afghanistan Wars did not stop a modern protracted war. In counter point, his war zeal in the 1960's and early 1970's did nothing but kill American soldiers in south-east Asia.

May the war profiteers burn in Hades. *Naturally, I'm just being satirical about the whole inferno thing. I hope war-profiteers just go on making pointlessly-long wars that murder Americans.* Please find the appropriate sarcasm in this paragraph. As a hint, I made the sarcasm in italics. The honest stuff has no italics.

This, however, was college life for Grover Glenn Norquist.

Free from the burden of poverty, combat, and any difficulty what-so-ever.

This same immature guy is defining America. Norquist decides how the Republican Party behaves. The guy intimidates and owns anybody stupid enough to sign his Pledge. It's like the Norquist Pledge makes the GOP the Persephone of our time. The GOP was snatched away by Hades-quist and tricked into signing the Pledge — thus causing frigid gridlock in the Congress and Senate forever.

95% of Republicans have signed The Norquist Pledge. This includes Bachmann, Cruz and other GOP'ers that might snipe at Norquist on TV — but they still signed his pledge.

The most difficulty Norquist ever had in life is the:

> *"Nixon fund-raiser people hassled him about his long hair."*
>
> *"But they backed off."*
>
> *"That was the brief hiccup in my participation in American politics."*

Oooo. So defining. That is exactly like taking point on patrol in Vietnam. You know, the guy who had to put a white X on his back so the guy behind could follow point through the jungle. The G.I.'s whose expected life span in combat was 10 to 14 minutes, if he was a pilot it was 12 to 17 days, and if he was stationed in the DMS around 2 to 5 months.

Long hair? Really. I don't know about that. The oldest picture I can find of Norquist is from the 1980's and he looked like this:

Not exactly the long haired hippy type.

I'll allow the '*long hair*' hippy struggle that so defined young Norquist for the moment. However, I would REALLY like for somebody to dig up a picture of Norquist in college. I betcha Norquist is a liar. I wonder if he even served as president of the Harvard Republicans?

Who knows?

• • • •

Grover Norquist has SO much insight, experience and understanding to offer the nation. Naturally, he should be the 'single most defining person for the platform dogma of the Republican Party.' *(egotistical quote from his own website)*

He did do one thing other than chair the College Republican Party during his college years.

He was a Hasty Pudding Theatrical member. This is a long standing Harvard student society — best known for its burlesque cross-dressing. No girls allowed. Men do all the parts.

Grover Norquist must have looked stunning in his pumps as he danced in a frilly corset — while other men were drafted and wore combat boots and fatigues.

Did the cross-dressing mature Grover or did he stay true to his twelve year old self?

Yep. Everything a man needs to know about politics he can form at twelve years old.

> **"I was active in the presidential race when I was 12 or 13. I worked on the Nixon campaign in 1968. I filed 'Get Out the Vote' cards. This is how old I**

am: These were 3-by-5 cards with addresses and people's names on them.

This was what he says he took away from College:

> **"When I became 21, I decided that nobody learned anything about politics after the age of 21. Look at people who grew up in the Great Depression, and their understanding of politics is Hoover and FDR. Fifty years later, everything is Hoover and FDR."**

Naturally, Franklin Delano Roosevelt, the President who got America out of a Great Depression, and led America to Victory while simultaneous fighting a World War — knows NOTHING about politics.

FDR was too old and mature to understand politics.

Twelve year old Grover has the real answer. Precocious, precious little boy.

So those old, stupid people who lived through the Depression and World War II don't know anything about politics.

Correct political opinions are fully formed by twenty-one.

I'm not buying any of Norquist's B.S.

Grover Norquist is an immature, selfish, bully.

Only cowards continue to surrender their own strength to this egotistical pre-pubescent man-child.

Hear that 95% of the GOP? Hear that Tea Party Caucus zealots?

You are cowards who follow the ideals of a man-child.

Grow up and stop following the ideas of a twelve-year-old.

Be mature already. Think for yourself.

RISE OF THE LITTLE DICTATOR

CHAPTER 6

Transparency is just for the little people.

So, how did an immature guy, with little life experienced, and a silver spoon, come to define the GOPs party platform?

How did a spoiled, narcissistic, pudgy-McPudge decide that the rich shall have no taxes, and the poor shall have no support?

Grover Norquist's view of government is sociopathic. He would make serial killers grin with his famous ideal. Quoth Norquist:

> *"My goal is to cut government in half in twenty-five years, to get it down to the size where we can <u>drown it in the bathtub</u>." – Grover Norquist*

If people cannot see that '*drowning*' something small in a bathtub is psychopathic, I am sincerely concerned about humanity.

In fact, let's take a politics break to look at the minds of serial killers. A little CSI time...

"Power Seeker Killer — a person who enjoys having total control over the fate of their victim."

Hmmmm? Sound like anybody you might know in politics? Maybe somebody who wants to shrink the government down and drown it in a bathtub? Tea Party sociopaths, like Bachmann, who say it is a good day when the government has a bad day.

Maybe I'm a little over the top with the whole '*Norquist is a killer*' thing. But, he really is doing a great job killing the Republican Party along with the nation. It's ironic he longs for small government and is murdering his own minions to get there, just like a James Bond supervillain who kills his own henchmen in a fit of rage.

Okay. I agree. Serial killer is a bit too far even for a satirist to make. Let's brainstorm about Norquist again.

The proper psychological evaluation would be:

<u>Narcissistic Personality Disorder</u>

As in, *"Grover Norquist has Narcissistic Personality Disorder."*

Did you notice that Norquist and Narcissist rhyme? No? Well, now you do. Is this just an accident or a cosmic mandate?

Let me see what WebMD has to say about Narcissistic Personality Disorder:

> Narcissistic personality disorder is further characterized by the creation of an anti-tax lobby, an abnormal love of self, an exaggerated sense of superiority and importance, and a preoccupation with success, power and getting Republicans to sign a treasonous pledge. However, these attitudes and behaviors do not reflect true self-confidence. Instead, the attitudes conceal a deep sense of insecurity and a fragile self-esteem. People with narcissistic personality disorders also often have a complete lack of empathy for others — and want to drown little stuff in bathtubs

Okay so I added slightly to this definition. Still, it fits.

● ● ● ●

Seriously, let me continue with some real traits of Narcissistic Personality Disorder. I promise I won't Norquist these up. They are complete:

In many cases, people with narcissistic personality disorder:

- Are self-centered and boastful
- Seek constant attention and admiration
- Consider themselves better than others
- Exaggerate their talents and achievements
- Believe that they are entitled to special treatment
- Are easily hurt but may not show it
- Set unrealistic goals
- May take advantage of others to achieve their goals

Other common traits of narcissistic personality disorder include the following:

- Preoccupation with fantasies that focus on unlimited success, power, intelligence, beauty, or love
- Belief that he or she is "special" and unique, and can only be understood by other special people
- Expectation that others will automatically go along with what he or she wants
- Inability to recognize or identify with the feelings, needs, and viewpoints of others
- Envy of others or a belief that others are envious of him or her

- Hypersensitivity to insults (real or imagined), criticism, or defeat, possibly reacting with rage, shame, and humiliation
- Arrogant behavior and/or attitude

Are you kidding me!

This just described Grover Glenn Norquist to a Tee. My freshman year of college psychology really paid off in this book! High five Internet doctoring and my Intro to Psych class for such a stunning and difficult diagnosis of the Grover weirdo of politics.

Grover Norquist is just a lobbyist.

A lobbyist with NO citizenry vote.

Grover is a lobbyist with Narcissistic Personality Disorder.

So, this all begs the question on HOW did Grover get over 95% of Republicans to go along with him. Let's take a look at how successful the egotistical Norquist claims to be per his own website:

Today the Taxpayer Protection Pledge is offered to every candidate for state office and to all incumbents.
- 235 Representatives and 41 Senators (Nearly all Republicans except 1 Democrat weirdo)
- 30 State Governors
- 1100 State Office Holders

The website boldly proclaims: "*Signing it has become de riguer for GOP candidates running for federal or statewide offices across the country.*"

So, back to my question. How does a little bully get so many complacent minions?

He finds immature minds to support his power structure. How about the always infantile Ted Nugent for example? "Mr. Cat Scratch Fever...the first time that I got it I was just ten years old...I got it from the pussy next door."

That '*Pussy next door*' Ted Nugent LOVES Grover Norquist and this little advertising gem of adolescent-thought was splashed all over Norquist's Americans for Tax Reform:

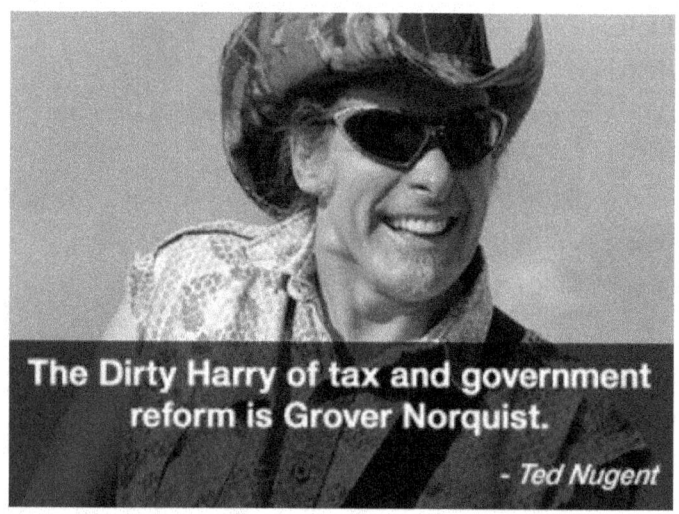

The Dirty Harry of tax and government reform is Grover Norquist.

- *Ted Nugent*

Go ahead, make my day. Sign up...

This little Norquist gem has all the proper elements of Grover's narcissistic, twisted anger.

A threatening under tone "The *Dirty Harry of tax and government reform is Grover Norquist.*" I can almost feel the gun glaring into my 'looter' face, as I'm promised "*Go ahead, make my day...*"

The Norquist ad is presented by a noxious, sophomoric, has-been star, Ted Nugent, who happens to be a big gun nut. (*I own guns. They are a tool. They are NOT my identity.*)

This simple, threating image also reflects the methods of how Grover Norquist controls 95% of the GOP, and therefore punishes the nation into acquiescing to his twelve-year-old point of view.

Quite simply, he controls the Republicans because they allow him to bully them by this complex formula:

1. If a GOP member refuses to sign The Pledge he/she is attacked in the next election by a well-funded GOP candidate who DOES sign the pledge.

That's it.

That's the entire complex vehicle that Grover Norquist uses to control the Republican Party, and destroy our great nation.

One step. Just financially back a Republican signer against a Republican that does NOT sign The Pledge.

Easy and deadly. It is killing the nation.

Norquist is proud of his vindictiveness too:

> "The pledge is not to me — exactly. It's to the voters that I steal in proxy. So an elected official who says, 'I think I wanna break my pledge,' he doesn't look at me and say that. For my eyes are like the sun! My gaze would melt his insubordinate face! He looks at his voters and says that.
>
> Some beg me upon bended knee and say, "Well, how 'bout you, my Malevolent Master? Could you release me from my pledge?"
>
> "No, no. I can't help you," I thunder down from lofty heights.
>
> I, King Norquist, remind voters which Republicans took the pledge. The voters retaliate because I spend a bazillion dollars (of Corporate money and fat cats) to punish that offending non-signer of The Pledge. I organize a specific attack campaign to send breakers of MY LAWS back to another line of work, like shoplifting or bank robbing, where they have to do their own stealing. (*I find it strangely humorous that Norquist thinks his minions are closely related to bank-robbers.*

Maybe this is why he can get them to sign in the first place? No morals.)

Once the voters obey my bidding... bahahahah... I applaud from the sidelines. I go, 'Very good. Yes, yes.'

Much like Mr. Burns of the Simpson Franchise. Mr. Burns is my personal hero."

Most of this dialogue is real text from a 60-Minutes interview with Grover Norquist. Perhaps, for comedic effect I made some minor modification? I dunno. Go watch the interview yourself if you want clarification.

● ● ● ●

So, do I have you on pins and needles to see this Pledge. It must be stunning in its complexity. It must be like a golden-fleece or the Excalibur of mythology.

(Please remember that this Pledge was drafted by a twelve year old, who never grew up in the slightest. I'm just the barer of disappointing news).

But BEHOLD! The Norquist Pledge!

This! Behold!

This Pledge is what is paralyzing the Nation. This is what is moving The United States of America ever closer to a huge recession.

There might be some who would say it is TREASON for any elected official to take a pledge to any lobbyist. There might be some who say the "Oath of Office" is the ONLY legal pledge for an elected official.

Hey! There is somebody who would say it. Me!

> "Signing the Norquist Pledge is Treason."
> – *Stephen Paul West*

Taxpayer Protection Pledge
I, _____, pledge to the taxpayers of the (____ district of the) state of _____ and to the American people that I will: ONE, oppose any and all efforts to increase the marginal income tax rate for individuals and business; and TWO, oppose any net reduction or elimination of deductions and credits, unless matched dollar for dollar by further reducing tax rates.

Do you think I'm being a bit extreme? Well, let me go back into recent history.

Let's say John F. Kennedy took a pledge to the Pope over the Oath as President?

Would that have been treason?

Yes. Yes, that would have been treason.

During JFK's election the nation was so serious about secret pledges and undisclosed allegiances that John Kennedy had to go on television and explain his affiliation to the Pope versus this country. He made very clear he could only legally and morally obey the Oath of Office. So, people relaxed and voted in the first Catholic.

But the Norquistites don't disclose their secret, contractual unholy bondage to Norquist and the *The Pledge of Power!*

Let's say you are a famous Revolutionary General. A hero. And suddenly you take a pledge to the British Crown. In that case, your name would be Benedict Arnold. The most famous traitor in American history.

Well, almost the most famous. 95% of Republican's are bigger cowardly rats, but Grover Norquist is the biggest Traitor of American History. May his name be consign'd to Obscurity.

As old Ben Franklin penned about Grover Norquist (I used my time machine and went back to see the man on the Five Dollar bill. When Ben found out, he drafted this notice!

Well, in defense of the signers of The Norquist Pledge, there is a more compelling Certificate of Pledge that I can see might dazzle them with its beauty.

Behold! The beautiful Certificate of the Pledge!

AMERICANS FOR TAX REFORM

United States House of Representatives candidates

Taxpayer Protection Pledge

I, _____, pledge to the taxpayers of the _____ district

of the state of_____, and to the American people that I will:

ONE, oppose any and all efforts to increase the marginal income tax
rates for individuals and/or businesses; and
TWO, oppose any net reduction or elimination of deductions and
credits, unless matched dollar for dollar by further reducing tax rates.

Well, this new picture of The Pledge is a game changer! No wonder why Republicans are lining up to put their name on it!

It kind of reminds me of something Napoleon once said:

> "A soldier will fight long and hard for a scrap of colored ribbon." – *Napoleon after destroying his own country.*

Grover Norquist found out exactly what Napoleon learned. Grover found out people will destroy their own integrity just to gather a little badge from some dictator.

Norquist's badge is The Tax Payer Pledge.

Norquist is the little dictator.

A traitorous dictator, but a dictator non-the-less.

It's time to vanquish this twit to a little island where he can look at himself in the mirror.

How complete is Grover Norquist's arrogance?

He demands complete transparency for all of his adversaries, but refuses to disclose who is funding his personal Lobby.

In fact, he is funded by corporations and by men like Jack Abramoff, the Ponzi con-artist who was the heart of a huge corruption case resulting 21 persons pleading guilty.

Grover Norquist laundered the illegal proceeds for Abramoff's stolen public dollars. Norquist used the *Americans for Tax Reform* lobby to illegally move the money into off-shores accounts.

Because of Norquist's strangle hold on the baby in the bathtub, the GOP investigators blocked any inquiry into their ad-hoc, treasonous leader.

THE FALL!

CHAPTER 7

Alas, poor Norquist, I knew him well.

The end of the line for our little despot glimmers ahead!

Grover Norquist's privileged life is not going to save him.

The last gasps of the dying Republican Party can't save him.

Norquist has made himself so small, that he is drowning himself in his own bathtub. He is taking the Grand Old Party with him.

Public Office is a pretty important American job.

Michelle Bachmann and the Tea Party Caucus swore allegiance to Grover Norquist. So did most of the other Norquist Republicans up for election.

(And really, shouldn't they be American Republicans? Why are they called Norquist Republicans. Answer: Because he owns their little biatch back-sides — — that's why.)

It is maybe, just maybe, a good idea to know the allegiance of the candidates applying for public position. It is important to know if the politician is too weird for the job, if he has a lying nature — and if he has a binding pledge sealed a conflict to the Oath of Office for that post. We The People actually have some expectation of loyalty from our elected officials. Really. I'm not just making this up.

The Constitution defines some of the duties of the politicians, and having weak sell-outs managing the nation's finances, tax structure, Nuclear affairs, Trade Agreements and the Political posts should make every real citizen afraid of Grover Norquist and his falsely named lobby organization.

I wish I could make this section satire, but it strikes me as too serious, unlike the con-artist hustle of the Reagan statues, and propaganda named Norquist projects.

Every elected official of Congress — both the House and Senate must make this pledge for office:

"I do solemnly swear (or affirm) that I

will support and defend the
Constitution of the United States
against all enemies, foreign and
domestic; that I will bear true faith and
allegiance to the same; that I take this
obligation freely, without any mental
reservation or purpose of evasion; and
that I will well and faithfully discharge
the duties of the office on which I am
about to enter. [So help me God.]"

-     *NOT the Norquist Oath of Office*

Where does any of this oath mention Grover Norquist?

The Norquist Pledge is Treason.

Plain and simple.

The good news is the tide is turning.

A few brave GOP members realize they were coerce or deluded into signing this foolish paper, and have renounced their neurotic leader outright.

A few brave GOP members never signed such a stupid piece of paper. These are perhaps the true heroes.

Grover Norquist managed to co-opt the image of Reagan with his statue program, and by this silly maneuver stole Reagan's image for his personal gain.

Imagine that I appointed myself to put Lady Gaga statues in every county in the United States. After a while, I would become the unofficial voice of Lady Gaga.

This connection to Reagan cannot be understated for Norquist's success. It is sad that humans can be so easily manipulated, but it is also in our nature.

Grover Norquist stole Ronald Reagan's physical presence with a thousand statues, and blended it all into a hob-goblin kind of authority. Grover is the jester who made himself king of the Republicans.

It is sad that some soldiers incorrectly fight and die for mere scraps of ribbons for a bad dictator. So, there are many GOP members who still doggedly embrace this treasonous pledge.

However, the citizens are coming alive.

Investigative news articles and amusing and tragic interviews with Norquist are exposing him for the narcissistic bully that is his defining character trait.

In the last election, Grover Norquist ran around like a petulant child on Fox News denying the loss of his personal Presidential candidate.

More stunning was tremendous turn-over of certain Republican seats to Democrats.

Certainly, Republicans with juvenile understanding of how a woman's body works, might still love Norquist. The same guys that justify *'legitimate rape'* and other foul and nefarious ideas.

Every one of them wears the same taint as Norquist.

Still, Grover Norquist is the consummate Narcissist. He doesn't even perceive his ideas are ridiculous. He has a threat aimed at any Republicans who dare throw off the shackles of THE PLEDGE.

The Norquist walks onto national television and issues his edict:

> *"We've got some people discussing impure thoughts on national television. I will find them. I have a particular set of Harvard skills that I've acquired over a lifetime of privilege. I will find them and I will kill them.*

> *Most likely by making them so small I can drown them in a bathtub."*

Let's all just keep voting against his candidates. Let this little tyrant wander off to an island somewhere so he can't hurt Lady Liberty any longer.

The nation should never negotiate with terrorists.

The nation should not surrender to the tyranny of 49 Tea Party Caucus politicians.

The government shutdown was pointlessly cruel.

Grover Norquist, Michele Bachmann and all Tea Party Caucus Republicans should be thrown out of Washington and politics.

Then America can get to work fixing any problems instead of making problems worse.

The End

● ● ● ●

BONUS HISTORY LESSON! Find all the similarities between Rural Electrification Act of 1935 and the Affordable Health Care Act of 2013:

The story of the Tennessee Valley Authority starts with Muscle Shoals, a stretch of the Tennessee River where the river drops 140 feet in 30 miles. That drop in elevation created the rapids or "shoals" that the area is named for and made passage farther upstream impossible. The federal government acquired the land in 1916, with the intent of constructing a dam that would generate electricity needed to produce explosives for the World War I effort, but the war ended without a dam being built.

In the following years, efforts were made to sell the land back to the private sector. Senator George W. Norris of Nebraska fought to keep the land in public ownership, but his efforts to have it developed were defeated by the resistance of Republican administrations. Calvin Coolidge vetoed one bill in 1928 and Herbert Hoover vetoed another in 1931 who took a hard-line position that:

> *The real development of the resources and the industries of the Tennessee Valley can only be accomplished by the people in that valley themselves. Muscle Shoals can only be administered by the people upon the ground, responsible to their own communities, directing them solely for the benefit of their communities and not for purposes of pursuit of social theories or national politics. Any other course deprives them of liberty.*

The election of Franklin D. Roosevelt altered the balance of power and finally led to action. On May 18, 1933, President Roosevelt signed the Tennessee Valley Authority Act,

America – the entire nation – finally became electrified; against the wishes of hardline conservatives.

• • • •

Stephen Paul West is a bestselling author living in Austin Texas.

Bibliography of Best-Sellers Include:

Top Ten Cures for Sciatica and Back Injury - Healing at the Speed of Read! Fix your back pain fast.

A list of ten 'must haves' to cure sciatica and back pain. Recovery from lower back pain and injury is difficult. This short self-help book presents the most powerful and effective ways to get pain relief fast! It is the ten best cures to recover from lower back injury and sciatic.

Nothing demoralizes and hurts like back pain. I should know. After a criminal ran me over and left me for dead, I developed repeated incidents of back pain that left me bed-ridden for days, weeks and occasionally months. I found the tricks and tips that work! So, I truly believe you can and WILL have a vibrant recovery.

"Top Ten Cures for Sciatica and Back Pain" is a skill builder to speed the recovery from back pain. Back injury impacts over 90% of people in their life — and few injuries have a more negative impact on human quality of life than back pain. This book is full of the best tricks to get you off the bed and back on your feet!

There is no rocket science in this short work. It is designed to get right to the point and help you get over your back pain.

The definitive guide to fixing back injury

Depression Symptoms Decoded – a deep analytical look into the meaning of depression symptoms. Depression symptoms are a body's immune response to emotional damage, and the cure for depression is to understand the meaning of the symptoms displayed. This self-help explorers the body's method to heal emotional injury and this includes Weeping, Sex Issues, Recurrent Dreams, Rage, Isolation, Fatigue, Confusion, Addictions, Appetite Changes and Dark Thoughts/Suicide. **Warning for Mature Language and Dark Situations**

The Peace of Gaza – Shocking. Stunning and Beautiful, This is the most powerful short story of our time. Prepare to be touched to your core. Three souls wander the very place where twenty years earlier the world was ending. Twenty years after the world narrowly avoids a nuclear holocaust coming from Gaza.

Rise of the Maiden (Blood and Venom Series) - Craving something new and sophisticated in the paranormal genre? In the first years of the reign of Victoria, an infant girl is stolen from the dirty streets of London. For fifteen years she is held an unknowing prisoner by the captor she calls 'father'. The mystery is deep, dark and very gothic. **Warning for Mature Content**

Mitt Romney Too Weird to be President (and Why) - Mitt Romney really is too weird to be President. This quick read takes a hilarious, satirical and informative romp through the mind of this Presidential wanna-be. There is something afoul with Mitt when Hitler ends up in heaven, Afro-Americans are thought to be cursed by Cain (and really how many minority members does Mitt Romney have? I can count them on one hand even if four fingers are cut off); Women give men power with God by having kids; and a half dozen kooky ideas that form the vows of this high priest of Mormonism.

Arms Stronger Than War – A woman exists always, but a mother is made only the moment her baby is born.

What would you do to save your baby in the horrors of modern war? A true story. A biographical-fiction base on three women who were caught in modern civil wars. Motherhood on the point of extinction. Modern warfare has no rules, no honor, and everywhere women pay the highest costs for their children. A woman exists always, but a mother is made only the moment her baby is born.

What would you do to save your baby in the horrors of modern war? Prepare for a book that will move you to the core.

• • • •

Dedication

Who Needs a Functional Government?
Certainly Not We The People

I dedicate this to all the politicians who believe their ideology is more important than democracy. Certainly, the crew of troglodytes who shut down the Federal government make for easy satire. Their absolute failure makes easy writing and this helps pay my bills – which is ironic because they aren't letting the nation pay its bills.

So, in a way, I need to thank those narrow-minded and stubborn 49 people plus Grover Norquist who make for easy satire, and easy money. I just hope I have an economy left in which to spend my earnings.

These taskmasters know best.

Thanks a Bunch

• • • •